Forthcoming by Robert Rowe

THE RAZOR, a novel about skiing (June 2020)
THE PERFECT SEARCH and other poems (January 2021)

Also by Robert Rowe

GARAGE SONGS, a novel (2018)

The Day Kal Aikens Streaked Down Main Street

and other poems

by Robert Rowe

Bellhorn Press
Wellesley, Massachusetts
2019

****

Copyright © 2019 by Robert Rowe
All rights reserved
Printed in the United States of America

No part of this book may be reproduced or shared in any form or by any electronic or mechanical means, including information storage and retrieval systems, without permission in writing from the publisher, except by reviewers, who may quote brief passages for purposes of a review.

ISBN 978-1-949064-01-8
Library of Congress Control Number: TBA
Design Editor: Jose Lucas, stargazingstudio.com
Front cover design by Kailey Torres
Rear cover design by Lewis Agrell
Author photograph by Holly Hinman
Editors: Michael Jones and Joan Crothers

Bellhorn Press
New Voices in Poetry Series
P.O. Box 812142
Wellesley, Massachusetts 02482
Phone: 781-214-0425

Publisher: Michael Jones.
Contact: mjones@bellhornpress.com
To order copies, please email: info@bellhornpress.com
To order copies for libraries and schools, please contact:
libraries@bellhornpress.com
For author readings and appearances, please email:
media@bellhornpress.com
Visit bellhornpress.com for more information.

This book is a work of poetry. Names, characters, places, and incidents either are products of the author's imagination or are used fictitiously. Any resemblance to actual events or locales or persons, living or dead, is entirely coincidental.

10 9 8 7 6 5 4 3 2 1

First Edition

****

For Marisa, my true friend and lover, my partner though holiday and rain, sunshine and funeral, without whom this book would not exist.

For Dewey who once ate 52 Fig Newtons and three pizzas during a single episode of "Six Million Dollar Man." The sick unit who launched six helicopters and three backscratchers in the bumps on the Golden Smelt. The kid who studied piano to learn one song, then quit, but still plays "The Entertainer" at parties. The self-proclaimed "Greatest of all time," who very well might be.

For Nancy Tokarz, shih' teacher, who assigned our 5th grade class essays on Rembrandt, Van Gogh, Michelangelo, Homer, and Renoir that opened up the unimagined world.

Table of Contents

The Last Time Marcus Muller Skied Tuckerman's Ravine   1
Chasing Fireflies Beneath a Funeral Sky   3
The Day Kal Aikens Streaked Down Main Street   5
The Red Sox Curse   8
Launch Me   12
The Rose Guitar   14
The Perfect Search   18
The Panic of 2008   26
The Geography of Music   30
Haunted House   32
Alien Planet Theory   37
Brush Cutting on Bitterroot Ridge, Montana   39
Kip Kasper and The Morning Gas Disaster   42
My Brother's Grateful Dead Records   45
The Polar Bear Club   47
Evil Knieval   49
The Parent Season   50
Aunt Grace   54
Elvis Impersonators   57
Into The Untraveled   58
Ode To The Hanson Brothers From The Movie "Slapshot"   60
The Game Olin Timmins Missed the Open Goal   61
The Pretend Man   65
Eric Russo the "Italian Tank" From Burlington   67
Handing Out Apples on Halloween Night in Merriam Hill   69
Subconscious Thoughts of a Celtics' Fan   71
Christmas Caroling on Oars Island   72
The Night Liam McGarvey Egged Lexington   75
In Praise of Cheap Shots   77
The Wrong Guy   78
Strip Poker with the Carson Sisters   79

Scenes From The Dentist Chair   80
Traveling to Darian's   82
Brett Douglass Swims The English Channel   84
The Blue Sling   86
Conversations From a Barber's Chair   87
Freedom on The Fringes For Francis Layne (Le Poème Morte)   89

The Day Kal Aikens Streaked Down Main Street

and other poems

The Last Time Marcus Muller Skied Tuckerman's Ravine

We have to travel a century back
for a spring with this much snow,
mid-June when Marcus Muller
parked his rusty Saab by the granite lodge,
threw his skis on his shoulder
and trekked up the snowfields
in a stream of ski-team coats
and tie-dye shirts with a girl
his mom points the finger.
At the peak, as the white tin sun
bounced off the corn mush snow,
Marcus buckled his boots, clicked on his skis,
and watched the Colby Ski Team
perform razor turns on the slope.
"I'm gonna schuss the whole thing," he said.
"Spare me." Shawna rolled her eyes up
as skiers shrank to black bugs below,
but Marcus stabbed the snow
and dropped down the ravine
in a full-tuck Coach Quimby wished
he'd never taught. The sudden rush
of arctic air pressed against his
sun-cooked face, stomach pushed to ribs,
edges hissing, pants flapping like a sail
as the gaps between moments fused
into one thin line down the White Mountain.
At the base, Colby skiers turned their heads
to one human luge fired from a cannon.
Marcus's brain flashing: *Stop!*

but his orphan body latching on
to one carnival ride in the now.
The granite slabs hurtling forward,
picnic lunchers parting like the Red Sea
and Frisbees hung in mid-air
when the icy slope burst into
birch leaves and lupine blooming
every shade of bruised flesh.
The curious angle of Muller's odd grin,
for a second, not from New Hampshire:
no fist-bent nose, flashing blue lights,
or dead-end jobs. No speed limit signs
when all we ever wanted - was to fly.
Instead, the Kancamangus Forest opening,
crooked birches leaning,
fiddlehead ferns, granite slabs,
Shawna's curves, the Saab—everything
spinning and turning, blurring
then merging back to white.
The Colby students latch skis
to their Jeeps and comfort Shawna
mumbling like a scratched record,
having slid down face-first
like the rest of us: skiers in time
caught in destiny's undertow,
not knowing Marcus Muller
had already schussed Tuckerman's
Ravine and his K2s were soaring
way above this bald summit
in a place where the skin never cuts,
the neck never snaps,
and the snow never stays
this late in June.

Chasing Fireflies Beneath a Funeral Sky

Beyond the screen door's slam,
Past the porch light's crescent rim,
Over a damp lawn, jam jar in hand.
Through mother's garden, ankle deep
In pillows of earth, leaping where the
Crickets dare for diamonds in the oil air.
Chasing fireflies alone in an August night.
Chasing fireflies beneath a velvet sky.
My sister twisting in pajamas, waist-high in
Hay. Reaching for flying summer, the glints
In an inventor's eyes so frail they crush
In a bird's beak like spirits in our soft
Skin shells snuffed in a tin-can car. Push
The black bugs through the jar's entrance
Before a curtain drops. Feel the ash burn
In your chest. Feel the caramel moments
Stretch. Chasing fireflies alone in an
August night. Chasing fireflies beneath
A velvet sky. Thirty bugs swirling.
My sister pokes holes in the rim,
But in their bedside prison the captured
Insects dim. Their moments of dark lengthen.
"They will not last the night," Aunt Bee warns.
"But we've circled the field for hours?"
Bee sips her Bloody Mary. "What's a
Fleeting moment worth?" In the field
We shake them free. They fall to earth,
Then struggle up a blade of green,
And back to the night release. I guess,
All fire wrestled from the sun's mouth

Visits for one brief evening.
Beyond the screen door's slam,
Past the porch light's crescent rim,
Leaping through a licorice night,
Chasing *ourselves* beneath a funeral sky.

The Day Kal Aikens Streaked Down Main Street

No one quite remembers
Where they were
The day before
Kal Aikens threw
His shoes in a bush
Behind First Trust,
Pulled off his shirt,
Slipped from his pants
And burst into
The busy sunlight
Down Main Street
Whooping like a
Movie Indian naked
Save a Halloween mask
Galloping through
The center of Bath
Flashing his lonely
Possession like a child
With an ice cream
Running the red light
Passing parked cars,
Too young to wait for signs.
The old ladies in line
At the Butcher's Block
Still question what they saw:
"Some kind of tan
Suit," they say smiling
As the noon sun drops
On rows of Fords
Still waiting for green,
On mothers pushing strollers

To the town clock's tick,
Kal's elbows and knees treading air
Like a scribbled comic character.
Passing Taylor's IGA
Kal made his first mistake:
Turning to the glass
He waved to a cashier
All of Bath knew
Was Kal's girl. By the library
Students resting from their books
Cheered. For the first time
Wind brushed the moon beam skin,
Touched the track team thighs
That boys began to chase:
A soul's mock escape
From a flesh prison.
Blinded by the salt
Kal tore off his mask
And beamed a thirty-tooth grin
Like he'd dethroned
The Russian hockey team.
"Where were the police?"
The mayor would later ask.
Sergeant Swan cruising for a
Donut as Kal crossed the street
Flashing Nixon's farewell salute.
Running behind Riddle's Drug
Where he made his last mistake:
The blue Dodge van,
The only one in town.
Engine left on, friends pulling skin
Too young for crow's feet
Inside. Tires skidding,
Kal's chest surging for air,
Unanchored with the future,

Drenched with desire
To sprint the Serengeti Plains
The way Jesse Owens did:
In the Führer's face.
The fiercer the sun —
The cooler the shade.
Kal's attempt to inscribe the moment
With *his* initials, to shed
The cloth distance between us,
To unplug the silent film
Running reel into reel
Into reel into real.
Folks around here still mark the time
The town clock stopped.
The day Kal Aikens
Streaked down Main Street
and never got caught.

The Red Sox Curse
(1918-2004)

Prelude

Even Oedipus couldn't
lose four World Series in a row,
all in the seventh game,
allow a GQ shortstop
a blue moon home run,
and auction off the Sultan of Swat
to finance a play time forgot.
Now the Babe lives forever
in pinstripes and crows pick the livers
of the Fenway parishioners.

Part 1

Dad's yelling at Mom again
as the vacuum roars across our den.
Mom insists, "The game's over."
Dad clutches a high ball
and screams, "Yogi Berra!"
I get the feeling we're on Nantasket
with plastic shovels and a sandcastle,
waiting for the high tide.

Part 2

It's August and Stanley is throwing
meatballs. They're rolling off our plate
and into the dog's mouth.
"Potato famine," Grandma yells.
Dad's speed feeding with two forks,
trying to get back to the eighth inning.

Mr. Yawkey, what are we to do now
in the fall with Cardinal leaves blazing?
Even with Yazstremski's Triple Crown,
the Impossible Dream was an ice cream
truck that never stopped in Beantown.

Part 3

The phone rings. It's my sister Doots.
She's "bailing" from her husband.
Too many "all-night sales meetings."
"Well," Dad clicks the TV on, "you can
always come home if you can stand
your moth—swing, dammit!"
Dad's highball splashes on his lap
as Evans takes another strike.

Every spring our hopes rise
like hairs on rookies' heads,
the webbed gloves, chalk lined fields,
and Dad's briefcase. Again
we swing for Cooperstown.
Again the pitcher turns his head.
Again we try to steal.

Part 4

"Can't we get along for one meal?"
my sister asks. Dad and Donk shoving
in the kitchen. Grandma's Noritaki cracking.
"Don't hit him," Mom screams.
The Splendid Splinter's barber pole swing,
born to pass the Babe, then
whisked away for Europe's war.
There's a lamp on in the kitchen.
Dad's combing through his ledger,
pounding a calculator.

Part 5
Then in eighty-six with Hurst hurling
the twelve deeds of Hercules and

Henderson like Captain Kirk discovering
the last minute miracle, we were so scared
the Sox would bust The Curse
and leave us alone in the loser's circle
waiting for our chance to bat.

But one glove from glory, one swat
from Fisk, one tug from Little,
the ball rolled past Buckner's Greek heel,
past Dad's vacant store, past Doots' wedding vows.
Rolling through time like our family tree,
across Storrow, down the Charles,
and out in the Atlantic where all strikes go,
even hits, and we return to some
providential order greater than one town.

Part 6
It's 4 a.m. and Chief Swan's at the door.
Mom's crying. Dad's nodding.
I run to my brother's room.
His sheets are flat as home plate;
The stoic Tiant faced Concepcion
like André faced the noose
but couldn't slow the Red Machine.

Still Doots dates, I rake the fallen
leaves of October, and Mom pays
the mortgage, hoping somehow
a tan Chevrolet pulls in our driveway
with Dad's hand dangling five tickets.

Part 7
Every morning I pull on my red socks,
slip down the stairs, and scan scores
in *The Globe* for some evidence of grace:
a left fielder reaching for a deep drive;
a pitcher who, for once, could place the ball
right where he wanted; for St. Francis the ump
who's known to overlook a few strikes.

A JFK speech, Flutie Hail Mary,
or Sam Adam's rabble-rousing:
some glowing series of notes
that might unlock the gates to
Cooperstown. I hear there's a new
shortstop who stretches singles
into triples, a fireballer who knocks
catchers over, and in Pawtucket
a new Babe whose parting shots soar
way above the Green Monster,
far beyond Boston Harbor,
out past the pock-faced moon
to unknown places by the stars.

And maybe that stitched ball
latches onto a comet's tail,
one that comes every thousand years,
and carries us away.

Launch Me

Bottle rockets in my socks,
run through a field but can't lift off.
Five umbrellas in my hands,
leap off a bridge but quickly land.

I swear this time I'm not afraid.
Been up all night with my razor blades.
I carve the wood and I squeeze the glue.
I'm flying after you.

So launch me, launch me,
launch me with my paper wings.
Launch me, launch me,
high above the trees.

Bed springs duck-taped to my shoes,
a diving board nailed on my roof.
In my chair with nine balloons,
the helium will lift me soon.

I swear this time I'm not afraid.
Propeller's carved and the rudder's made.
I thread the wires and turn the screws.
I'm flying after you.

So launch me, launch me,
launch me with my paper wings.
Launch me, launch me,
high above the trees.

I bet my parents will be proud
to see me soar above the clouds.
They'll call my uncles on the phone
and say I've hollowed out my bones.

I swear this time I'm not afraid.
When I land there'll be parades.
I'll gather speed across my roof
and lift my airplane in the blue.

So launch me, launch me,
launch me with my paper wings.
Launch me, launch me,
high above the trees.

I wish that they could see me go;
I'm flying off to I-don't-know.
I'll settle on an old-time farm
if I could learn to flap my arms.

The Rose Guitar

Nunny's shoveling words into my ears again,
something about Roosevelt's character.
It's Christmas Eve and we're singing by the piano,
but Nunny's howling about Harold's canary,

or is it Lilly fleeing from the tonsil man?
I've heard each tale a trillion times.
Nunny's hand is grasping a cane,
but her mind is leaping decades

to my brother Donk running through her attic
towards a group of boys, trying to halt a spider
execution. At nine, I'm not sure what her stories mean,
when jello neurons crystallize to quartz

and Nunny wears each synapse like a pearl
necklace. All I want to do is run
to my brother's room and steal his G.I. Joe,
but Nunny yanks me back to World War One

when German soldiers board her ship, and Nunny,
only five, hollers: "I think the English are nice!"
On the couch, Dad and Uncle Jim argue about Reagan,
Aunt Grace and Donk are on the floor arm wrestling,

but Nunny's hobbling around the den waving
Teddy's *big stick*. "Harold was built like a tank,
but when his canary died... 'I'll come straight home,'
his voice wavered on the phone." After pecan pie
we're drying dishes, but Nunny's plate's still full.

She's giggling at the table. "The local doctor
lined up the neighborhood kids to snip
their tonsils, but Lily climbed through a window,
leaped off the porch, and hid in the boathouse."

At twelve I ran from Nunny's guitar,
though she gave lessons for free.
In college, I made a detour around her chair
to drink Guinness with my cousins. At thirty,
I listened for a sec then switched on the Sox.

The Christmas Eves gave way to New Year's Days,
February snows to Bunker Hill parades.
Nunny's back bowed like a bamboo rod
reeling in a phantom fish. Then in May, Stop-n-Shop
phoned. Nunny was roaming in the isles, lost

among the canned peaches and maraschino cherries.
That Thanksgiving no one told stories.
Time's tourniquet kept the unsaid syllables inscribed
in our skulls, but there were stories Nunny never told:

The day Harold was driving through Scarsdale,
a Buick tried to pass, Harold yanked the wheel hard,
then glass, steel, and Harold went rolling down a hill.
How in '41 with two girls and a nurse's cap, Nunny
poked IVs, scribbled vital signs, and emptied bedpans.

At times, showered with bills and leaking roofs,
Aunt Grace found Nunny huddled in the kitchen,
or thirty years later on Mass Ave in Woburn,
a Blazer missed a red light but got Donk's Nova.
That night in the trauma ward, the only time I saw
her speechless. Though years earlier she told me:

when Truman faced a landslide, he mustered every ounce
of Missouri optimism and took a train across the country,
or after Grant lost the first Battle of Shiloh,
he muttered in his tent: "Whip 'em tomorrow."

How surprising to find that *we* were running
from the tonsil man, *we* were mouthing
off to German soldiers, my brother sprinted through
the attic and swept a daddy long-legs off *our* fingers;

that before Lincoln won the White House,
he lost the Senate; before MacArthur took
Okinawa, he ran from Bataan; that for every
Mickey Mantle home run, there were sixteen whiffs.

Now I know the secret to a great tale:
It is the vein of silver in a granite cliff,
in a crowd of ash faces—the splash of cherry lips,
the sun-stained shoulders on a blackbird's wing,

a '58 hollow-body Gibson that holds something
you didn't think could be held. Nunny strummed
her rose guitar and lured a flock of ruby-faced
finches back from a meadow of silence.

Now, I am too old to don a white sheet
and chase my grandkids down the street,
too old to argue why Roosevelt deserved
a third term or Patton should have toppled Stalin,
too old to stuff a football up my shirt
and sneak past the boys for a touchdown.

A grandson bolts past me with a truck in his mouth.
"Hey, Connor, come over here," I wave.
"Did I ever tell you 'bout the time in Hancock Church,

your Dad, Uncle Mike, and I, in cotton beards
played the Three Wise Men?
'Lay off the pop,' Dad warned,
but Bucky drank six sodas at breakfast
and mid-way through the service
he sprinted off the stage."

Laughing to myself, I open my eyes to an empty room.
In the dining room, silver forks clink against porcelain plates.
In the den grandkids sit cross-legged—spellbound by TV,
the rug is covered with crumpled gift wrap,
and our Christmas tree droops with glowing bulbs.

The Perfect Search

Part 1. The Tug of War

    Spellbound by the stadium's cheers,
I never heard the ants marching to a distant feast,
the improv genius of frog songs,
or swansong regrets to a bedside priest.

    My heels wedged in sand,
I never saw the lichen maps on Puritan graves,
the African masks on a moth's wings,
or blue-browed albatross camber the waves.

    With my biceps flexed,
I guided our canoe through the Everglades,
but came out with my canteen filled with swamp.
Still, I held on.

    In my captain's crewneck,
I waited for opponents to slip. I did not expect
the fresh legs of rookies or coaches' stirring sermons.
Both teams pulled, but the flag stayed even.

    "Have you thoughts of dropping this rope?" I asked
a helmsman. "And drift the sea without an oar," he said.
"Do you feel a submerged sense of loss?"
"Sometimes one forgets an attic's contents."

    What was the grand thing asked for?
I played my cards as a few grownups before:
an uncle who loved lasers, an aunt who chants
on straw mats. With those maps, I dug in my heels,

jawed with opponents, and never dropped my shield.
I toss all my bronze coins, even if there be no gold!

   In the August twilight a veteran spoke:
"I've heard of cliffs near Kovic where men have run
like school boys from a cherry bomb."
My pine-pitch hands released the rope,
from the stadium I ran, and like a cannonball
I dropped into the ghost-green sea.

Part II: The Baffin Sea

   A whitecap climbed above my head.
My body rose with every wave and fell in every trough.
With two eyes for a compass and a wet mouth for my companion,
I kicked the breaststroke east, swam the sidestroke south.
On all sides gray triangles poked the horizon.

   Out of the plum-dark sea with rhythmic blows,
white-throated killer whales surfaced
and took measure of me with their small knowing eyes.

   With Perseus as my pilot, I swam through winter.
In spring I greeted Pollux. In autumn bid adieu to Corvus.
Weren't there islands off Greenland with hillsides of lupine?
"You nitwit," I thought as my frozen limbs
pulled me from the surface. "You left the stadium to drown."

   I sank to Baffin's bed, resigned to the clock's last tick.
Gone this manic squirrel in a grade school vest.
Gone the glazed russets of a lost Easter.
Gone my ice pick notions to climb Everest.
I am more or less my father. So be it.
I'm a fingerling in the cold Atlantic. Who gives a tin tit.

    Shedding my captain's crewneck,
I paddled past the bulbous eyes of cod
and colonies of quahogs clamped in their shells.
Half-held in the umber, a mannequin rested,
arms pulled from its sockets. I saw a physics book,
its pages swollen and warped.

    A forearm down, I found a wedding band
and the gnarled fender from a banged-up roadster.
"The stadium isn't half-bad," I reconsidered.
I miss my nutbag friends and my kid brother,
always hanging his bum from a car."

    I drove my heels deeper (I admit, to push
for the surface) when my toe felt a steel case,
an inner-compass pointing to a sole harbor.
For the first time in each cell I felt the pale orbs;
I understood what drives an elm upwards
and tells a heal-all's braided gobs of dusk
to migrate towards the sun.

    With a pod of dolphins I rejoined the waves.
In full-butterfly I leaped above the scalloped crests
and dove in every trough. A child rises and a child falls.
"North," my inner-compass pointed
as my salty beard clipped the calcite caps.
The plum-dark Baffin, once narrow,
crooked, inward lanes of salt, now
the endless chambers of my trembling.

Part III: The Beach of Rain-Smoothed Stones

    A walrus dragged its body up the beach
through a rook of penguins. My inner-compass
scanned the tongue-flat stones. From a gray billion,

I tried to divine, not surface or nearness, but the lever,
not cousins or friends, but pure forms from
the Shadow Queen's hands. My newfound needle madly spun.

    With the usual degree of guesswork,
I stuffed a couple pounds in my trousers,
then hiked through a field of red-hot pokers
to the Humbermouth Grange,
where on Sundays they hold a ballroom dance.

    Inside the entrance Miss Crothers pinched
the knots in my neck, rubbed the arch of my foot,
then wiggled my jaw. She waved me away.

    Back in Burin a trawler chugged across the bay.
Slipping from my clothes, I threw myself on the beach,
rolled like an alligator, then peeled the sun-cooked stones
off my skin. I huffed-it to the grange.

    This time Miss Crothers, who also chairs
the garden club, asked the janitor to escort me
from the grange. He slipped me a piece of sea glass,
then drop-kicked me down the cedar stairs.

    In the bay a harbor seal poked its head through
the surf and watched me with his curious cue-ball eyes.
I poked at stones with my cane until the days
dissolved into a velvet night. First, Lyra
appeared with her chief star Vega,
twenty-six light years away. Then I noticed Deneb,
the grand dame of the Northern Cross,
only five-hundred light years off.

    Was it worth it? To search
for a chance savior when all my inner-chambers

can do is paint the world black? To one day wake
and discover joy had betrayed us? To fall
for the chorus in a teenage anthem:
"Don't Stop Believing." From my pocket
I pulled a handkerchief and waved it in the sky.
I closed my eyes.

    A wave nudged my thigh.
I woke with my head on a pillow of rain-smoothed stones.
I was unprepared to notice the hair-thin veins
of russet-milk quartz, flecks of tourmaline,
and pin-pricks of garnet. In a few gray
vessels, I saw smidgens of church-bell beryllium,
hidden whits of captain's-beard gypsum,
and lazurite the color of Norwich sky
made visible by eons of ghost-green waves
and a glacier's slow grind.

    With a few Pliocene stones in each hand,
I trekked through a field of flaming-lips
where a hummingbird hovers but goes nowhere.
I sloshed through St. Alban's bog towards the grange.
In the shell of a dead pine an arctic fox nursed her kits.

    Can I recompose the stolen notes
of my accidental self and launch my shoes
across a scarred gym floor where the unheard
melodies are floating through the air thicker than jam?
I walked past First Humbermouth Church.
"Purlee, purlee. Purlee, purlee," sang
a rose-breasted finch in a crooked birch.

Part IV: The Ballroom Dance

    Outside the grange the pilgrims linger,
though admission is free. Oh, some pass with rocks
from the street, but on the floor their knees bruise

their partner's, their heels scuff the soft pine boards,
with a squirrel's eye, they watch the other dancers.

    With a jeweler's eyeglass,
Miss Crothers studies my collection:
She measures each muscle's protraction.
With a baton, she mimics my rhythms of breath.
Consulting a torn chart, she diagrams my posture.
She nods.

    What strikes me as odd,
in the gym there are no spectators.
Purple Kiwanis Banners hang from the walls
and Rotary flags from all nations. In glass cases
brown basketballs and tarnished trophies
inscribed: "Spring Frolic 1943, Third Place"
and "Methodist League Champions 1958."

    I show my hand to a few dancers
and wait for a partner. In her hand, Marisa
reveals pinpricks of garnet and church-bell beryllium.
We shove off across the amber floor to the merry sounds
of Ken Wenning's Wolverine Band.

    On the floor no need to talk.
(I mainly speak from weakness.)
Shoulders squared, hands firm,
we begin our fine negotiation:
"Slow, slow, quick quick, turn."
"Slow, slow, rock rock, turn."

    In rhythmic sweeps across the gym,
pairs glide over the blonde boards.
"Slow, slow, quick quick, turn."
"Slow, slow, side-step, spin."
Chestnut hair, swan necks, heavenly bellies,

vanilla scoop breasts—unfrozen motion!
The silken couples carve the Humbermouth air.
In their wake, air sculptures spin off their bodies
across the pine floor, then vanish.

    Slow, slow, quick quick, turn.
Slow, slow, rock rock, spin.
Hips aligned, palms pressed, tangled fingers,
statues of wind fill the gymnasium,
then disappear, the residue of perfect gestures.
"Slow, slow, quick quick, turn."
"Slow, slow, walk walk walk, spin."
All we can do is carve another one,
and string the milk-glass pearls
from bassinet to frost-dust.

    In our stillness,
we taped on the brows of a monk,
but through our movement,
we stole the ragged shoes of a sage.

    The gym lights flicker.
I pop nitroglycerin like mints.
"There's time for one more," says Marisa.
"One more air sculpture made dear
'cause we blew our youth in the tug of war,
almost drowned in the Baffin Sea,
poked rain-smoothed stones for years,
and slogged through Nowheresville to get here."

Wider than an oil tanker we turn.
(Our last defiant act.) The onion-scent
of overripe flesh fills the grange. Dancers depart
in wheelbarrows pushed by janitors
with shovels. Some leave in mid-step,
some their hands still clinging to their partner's.

   I crumple to the floor. A janitor
scoops me up and wheels me from the gym,
beneath an exit sign, through a field
of trumpet vines, and tips me
into a rectangular hole by a row of apple trees,
then covers me with cinnamon dirt.

   It is June again in the aspens.
The hackberries, buckeyes, and cloudy wings
ripple above my bed. In a slanted ash
a gray frog flutters its musical trill:
"Preep, preep. Preep, preep."
Below in a brown acre of water,
a bullfrog replies (as if I never mattered):
"Jug-o-rum, jug-o-rum, jug-o-rum."

   What about the ants?
(I almost forgot about the ants.)
They form long unheard of lines,
not seen since the building of the pyramids
when the Jews pulled sandstone
through a desert for the pharaohs.
The ants are marching to where I lay.

Having traveled so far, waited so long
and come so close, the ants fear that
perhaps this distant feast
is only a mirage.

The Panic of 2008

    The hair-pulling begins
fifty-four floors up
in skyscraper boardrooms,
Wall Street credit-default
swap pirates launch Trojan horse
scud-missile derivatives
at teacher pension plans
and pipe-fitter unions,
while red-carpet, corporate chum
Alan Greenspan pisses
on his own dissertation
and preaches "self-regulation."
    Meanwhile, twelve floors below,
legions of ethically rudderless
Ivy League stockbroker popes
hang albatross mortgage-backed
securities around the necks
of coupon-clipping mothers
and retired town clerks.
    A taxi cab ride uptown,
on Knickerbocker Club
blackjack tables, a silent hand
is betting against the soul.
    Five blocks away, headless
ostrich, credit-rating whores:
Moody's, Fitch, let's not forget
S&P, green stamp financial
Hindenburg with triple-A ratings,
but downgrade Uncle Sam to
AA plus, hogtying Bernanke and
Geithner as they aim fire hoses

at crony capitalist inferno.
   Oh wait, there's more.
A hawk's flight away, the Four
Blind Mice: Deloitte, Ernst & Young,
Klynveld, and Price Waterhouse,
perform hocus-pocus, Repo 105,
mark-to-market horse theft
on corporate balance sheets,
hiding billions of distressed assets
and triple-dipped bond commissions,
so public pension fund know-nothings
and late-to-the-rally sheep
keep buying orange peels -
their centers already eaten.
   Zoinks! Take an Acela Express
south. Zucchini-green smoke
rises from U.S. Treasury printing
presses, running 24/7, crushing
grandkids with debt, consuming
hemp fields the size of Delaware
to raise U.S. free-market Titanic.
   In the captain's chair,
Goldman Sachs' mole Hank Paulson
covers dollar-for-dollar his firm's
1919 Black Sox bets, handing too-big-
to-fail Wall Street Frankenstein casinos
(and his Sigma Alpha Epsilon frat buddies)
a sixteen-trillion dollar lolly pop.
   Ho, ho, ho, twelve years earlier
on Capitol Hill, big-business ventriloquists,
lobbyist parrots U.S. Congress
and third-rate cheeseburger salesmen:
Gramm, Rubin, Leach, and Clinton,
toss Glass–Steagall's fifty-five year
winning streak in the trash,
splashing the gasoline called risk
on American economy.

    On September 15, 2008,
the scud missiles land, sprinkling
ghost-pepper hot sauce on the nuts
of American taxpayers. The inferno
of greed consumes: Lehman Brothers,
Bear Stearns, Countrywide, WaMu,
Merrill Lynch, and AIG, incinerating
three trillion dollars in 401(k)s, nine
million jobs, six million homes lost,
leaving government cheese
and mayonnaise sandwiches
with Kool-Aid for the 99%.
    Meanwhile, the 1% corporate officer
arsonists leap from their burning firms
with golden parachutes. Who was John
Locke? they never ask from their ski
chalets in Aspen. What did Nathan Hale
do? they never wonder as they wire
$200 million to their Panama lawyers.
How does Kant's categorical imperative
apply to *me, me, me*? is never heard
on the decks of their Taj Mahal yachts
cruising the Caribbean.
    From Long Island Sound
to Golden Gate Bridge, white collar
corporate pickpockets lift trillions
from Uncle Sam's trousers. Not one
buccaneer goes to prison. If you're from
Greenwich, no get-out-of-jail-free card
needed. Just a soulless Ivy League law firm
to hand out motions, injunctions, and delays
like a department store Santa Clause
until the SEC budget busts
and their clients pay a lousy fine.
    God forbid a Mattapan teen
steals a car or a Haight-Ashbury bandanna

grandmother sells an ounce of cannabis—
both get twenty years in Otisville.
    In the Panic of 2008,
the Dow falls off a cliff. China
encircles the ransacked City on a Hill.
Robo-signer foreclosure mills
kick six million families to the street.
In Central Park, gray squirrels scuttle past
the acorns and run off with the oak trees.

The Geography of Music

Do you know what it means to love music?
As a six o'clock sun rises above the treetops,
my Chevelle barrels towards a granite-domed
monadnock. I am dizzy to be wise.

At the trailhead, I hike into the woods. Along the trail,
fiddlehead ferns unroll their summer flags. In small
streams, swirling whirligigs spin off momentary circles.
Every instant a new series of notes emerges.

High in the krummoltz, the windswept spruce scratch my shins.
With each measured step, the gnarled trees grow closer to earth,
then the trails disappear. In the alpine zone, I walk along
the granite ridge line. The unheard melodies
are floating through the air thicker than jam.

Reaching the summit I sit on a boulder and study the lichen maps.
After the sun drags its tired face across the sky, star-stitched patterns
emerge in the dusk. Are they music? In distant pines, great horned owls
hoo as hikers huddle in their tents. Are they music? How can I tell
when every minute the true magnetic-north shifts? I know this:
before I am wise, I am a pilgrim. Before I find music,
beneath my ribs there is a thumping.

What is music? From tinhorn radio stations,
millions of disc jockeys are telecasting songs. Are they music?
On makeshift stages in Unitarian Church basements, dozens
of unsigned bands are improvising perfect sounds. Are they music?
Perhaps music is the shell of a scallop or a hollow-body Gibson
that holds something you didn't think could be held.

Uncle Walt says, "Music cannot be passed from one person
who has it, to another person who does not." I say, music
is a '63 Corvette split-window coupe with 2,327 parts,
all working at once, so the notes lift you up from one state
and plunk you down into another. So let the magnets sing
and lure the steel scraps from a hillside of spare parts and
piece together an ageless car that whisks us off to caramel time.

But how can we have music when everything we love
is swallowed back into the earth? A mint song is different.
After the last chorus, a mint song builds and builds.
It doesn't dip down like a drunk goose. No way.
It's not a deer in deep snow forging towards silence.
No chance. A mint song spirals upward in a colloid
of perpetual rising. In its final flurries, a mint song
builds and builds, then it *climbs,* then the track stops,
but in the distant post offices of your salmon flesh,
in the electric sea juice inside your skull,
and across the sonic freeways flowing
through the universe, the song never ends.

Haunted House

Part 1
My sister's curling her hair in the tub again,
stuffing empty cereal bowls under her bed.
My brother's raising tomatoes in the basement,
but they're not the "Big Boys" my parents think.
"Billy Graham what have I done?" Dad wonders
and tightens his tie in the closet mirror.

Part 2
Dewey's on the roof with his friends
seeing who can piss the furthest
and reach Grandma swimming in the pool.
Downtown Doots enters Spellman's Shoes
with Mom's stolen Visa. "Must have
done something in a past life,"
Dad mumbles in the driveway,
an evening Globe tucked under his arm.

Part 3
He knows Kristen's been glued
to a TV all day with twelve cans of Coke
and a year's supply of Fig Newtons.
He sees the blue rays pressed against
her windows as he side-steps the toys
strewn across our walkway.

Part 4
He wants to talk to her,
be the father one should,
but has an alarm clock in his head,
a shipment of Chevys to sell

in time to pay First Trust,
give the sales force their slice,
and still have enough for eight rounds
of clothes and Donk's medical bills.
Dad did the only way he knew how:
the way Grandpa had done
and Great-Grandpa before.

Part 5

"How much do you kids charge
to haunt a house?" Dad screams,
V.O. in hand, TV cranked to ten,
but still he hears Vicky in the kitchen
tap dancing to the ghost of Shirley Temple,
Mikey on the tops of crutches walking,
and Dewey in the basement strumming
heavy metal vomit.

Part 6

Dad must have glanced often at the curled
photo's wedged in his mirror: a high school
runner with his number taped to chest,
a choir boy with Grandma on the steps
of St. Luke's, an Army officer with
an uptight haircut, not yet knowing the
Taj Mahal up close is only a tower of sand,
the pyramid of Giza just a tombstone,
that Gandhi was a frustrated lawyer,
and Washington's stoic pose was
only wood teeth. Later, when Dewey
never came back from a ski trip,
how deeply Dad sank in evening's chair
and tried to change the channel.

Part 7
Our graduations marched on by.
Our tassels now only bookmarks.

Dad spends his days watching boys
crunch helmets, burning Camels,
and howling for a dinner that never
comes. Outside, the neighbor's kids
are climbing pines. Their hands scale
the bark trunk like Braille readers
now you see who they're reaching for.
You phone and wonder when we'll visit,
if once we believed in Lindbergh,
and could we face our beds, hold hands,
and ask to live those parts once more?

Part 8
How clearly we would see those cereal bowls
slipped under a bed drying like cement,
those carnival spirits peeing off the roof.
How we'd ask Donk to fetch a few tomatoes.
How we pulled hair, poked eyes,
kicked shins till Mom's van swerved.
How glorious Washington was at Yorktown
when the world turned upside down.
How much better it is to be a fool
than a silent one.

Part 9
You brother, you sister, you father:
all your faces stained in my mind
like the fruit-strewn streets in Haymarket.
How can you ever die? What passes when
a twelve-room home is sold for a three-room

condo? Each C in each exam, each recovery
from the flu, each time Doots dipped a knife
in ketchup and pretended to die,
Mom rested on a mountain of laundry
or patiently eyed the driveway at midnight.

Part 10
Now we know, Dad, that no trampoline
springs us from this haunted house,
but what seeps through, each invisible
envelope of joy, is enough
to make, even the shortest life,
a Mona Lisa. You Dewey,
catching an edge in the groomed snow,
sailing into the woods where the patrol
found you curled like a squirrel:
how did the world go on the next day?

Part 11
Tonight I drive home to my own kids,
tearing up the rugs with their tiny bikes,
scribbling crayon murals on the walls.
My part of town is a lot poorer
than you afforded, Father.
Driving past Kristin's house,
alone with her five cats,
wanting to stop but already late.
Electric rays are pressed against
her window. Still hiding in her room,
lost in the parade of eight kids.

Above each house, gray clouds hang
on winter branches like rags on an
ancient scarecrow - so many words unsaid.

How bright the moon pokes a hole
through my windshield as I lift my foot
from the gas and drift towards
the nearest driveway, thinking it's time
I pull over and talk with her.

Alien Planet Theory

Mother shook her finger
and chewed the steel strands
of her Beethoven hair.
Her indigo eye shadow
in vogue decades ago.
On every surface, piles
of unopened mail and stacks
of library books stained
with coffee rings.
Brushing bank statements
off a kitchen chair,
Mother calls: "Come here,"
and begins to brush my hair.
She stares at my face
the way a jeweler eyes
a diamond or a sophomore
Medusa trying to turn
the world to stone,
what Dad's early exit and
our open mouths had done.
Her Lucky Strike voice,
known to praise Nixon,
surprises me like the whiff
of our cat box. "Aliens have
lived on Earth since Olduvai
Gorge." She darts me a glance
and continues to brush.
"Your expressionless face reveals
an inner-smile—I know,
the truth is hardest to believe."
She coughs. "Like the wealthy,

they quietly give and take
paintings, profits, and men."
By the sink I see plastic tubes
like rolls of pennies inscribed
for her brown thoughts: *Take one.*
"When aliens are hungry they eat."
My hair ripped. "They conspire
for us false prophets and fruitless
journeys." She tightened her apron.
"There are many nations, but they
cannot perceive one another."
Mother lay down her brush. "I think
they hate." She kissed my head.
"You have a lovely almond-shaped
head like your dad." In the mud
room she zipped up my coat.
"Raise your hand in class today.
Let's the teacher know you're listening."
She handed me a lunch box
and opened the screen door.
"Now take this and run
or you'll be late for school."

Years later, while playing pick-up
basketball, I twisted an ankle
trying to pivot free. I pressed ice
to my wound and felt scales.

Brush Cutting on Bitterroot Ridge, Montana

"Flying waves of fire never thrilled me," I say.
"The safe will protect our photographs," my wife assures.
"But I care more about the house," I say.
She looks like she will explode.

"I can't tell how many, but many
years back we could see the whole canyon,
the Rattlesnake River too,
then the conifers inched up,
then the ponderosas--
Oh, what the hell, said the firs.

The sun dripped its magic juice
The wood ferns and saplings rose.
Only from the roof could we see
the peregrines floating in the sky.

At least we had the scent of moss rippling
through our curtains. But fire leaps a gulch
and runs a ridge, while Kendra and I,
unaware on the Blackfoot in a canoe
would return to charcoal cubes.

So we begin with tamaracks,
their pulp so close to wedding cake
that our blades freeze in sap.
Then, there's alder and ash.

We lop off their arms so red perillas
can live amid the needles and
lady's slippers even a moth could topple.

The snow cherries though,
draw the pain-in-the-ass jays.
The pine groves house the imperial woodpecker's
ceaseless hammerings and the hooded squirrels
that summon the floating shadows
whose talons lift up their wiggling legs.

"We must rake two-hands deep," I say,
"or all this springs back."
"My guess is it won't matter what we do,"
my wife says dousing a mound of branches with gas.

    A few careless campers drunk on Lawson's
Sip of Sunshine can reduced these canyons
to moonscapes. In August, we're ready for the granddaddies;
the lodge-pole pines with morels in their roots
and last century's burn marks on their sides.

The moist sawdust, sweet as blood,
leaves blond patterns on the forest floor.
My wife throws me to the ground
as a larch tips over. Ninety-three rings I count.
"When this larch took root,
Oma was in kindergarten," Kendra says.
"Taft was President," I say.
"More like McKinley," she says.

We wrap the trees in chains
and hitch them to our pickup.
Peat spits up from under our tires
as we drag the trunks to an ash pit.

In their wake, the ground is prepared for
the long robes of a holy man. A curious whitetail
watches, then arcs into the forest.

With each *Timber!* fresh sheets of sun
slant onto moss beds large enough for a tablecloth.
Wide patches of sky open for a boomerang
of geese. To the west, new distances are laid bare
to Grant Creek Ridge all the way to Olympia.

As the last crowns fall, the bowl of Rattlesnake
Canyon opens, sloping down to the banks
of the Big Blackfoot, then climbing on the tops
of pines up Bitterroot Ridge before lifting off
into big sky's blue ether, shoots of tangled sun
streaming in every angle, further than an owl
can see, in mild waves of wakefulness.

Kip Kasper and The Morning Gas Disaster

Our summer cabin packed as a matchbook.
Nieces, nephews, aunts and uncles asleep
on every table, rug, bed, and couch.
With the feathery foot of a dancer,
Kip Kasper tip-toes to the crapper
contemplating stomach cramps in the still dawn.
Stepping over pajama-clad cousins
and friends in sleeping bags snoring:
not one eyelash flutters.
Cursing the door hinge's upward climb,
gingerly raising the lid,
assuming the throne position,
Kip flexes posterior muscles
to muffle the infamous horn
to squirrel squeaks. Like Rodin's thinker,
he sits for hours dispensing pressure
in whistles like Grandma's coil heater,
but in his stomach the acid bubbles build
into Macbeth's wart-nosed witch's broth full boil.
"Charge!" The bubbles rush for the nearest exit
like Confederate cavalry sweeping up
Missionary Ridge. Kip squeezes
to halt the charging plebes:
"Damn the onion pie! Damn all Cherry Coke.
Damn the Doritos!" Kip flexes till his ears pop,
but the fierce cadets will not be denied.
Ask any 8th grade chemistry prof:
"Gas seeks open space to be defined."
"Bthaaaaarrrrrrooooommmmppppffffththhhh.
Puh, puh, puhththuuuggggthththuuuhhh,"
sounds the loudest fog horn

the Titanic should have had.
"Judas," he shrieks like a train's break.
Through the paper-thin door,
eyelids open. Guests begin to rustle.
In the kitchen, bacon sizzles.
Like surging Mount St. Helen's,
the soldiers mount another charge.
Kit bites his tongue and strains his cheeks
like Hans and Franz: "Ahhhh! Yahhhh. Ahhhh!"
Suddenly, the sound of a two-ton lady
surfing on a plastic couch:
"Purrrtharruuuuummmphffffaaaththhhhh."
Triton's horn rocks the walls
the way house music shakes Zoots: "Shuuuushe-
shusheeeththawwweeeeesh, puh, puh,
theeeeeewhaaaaaapuuuuthththth."
Kip's face assumes the color of a grape.
From the bathroom oozes the odor of sardines
and dead dolphins on the beach.
"Who's in there?" a laughing friend hollers.
Kip purses his lips hoping silence will dispense
the moment. The cabin stirs with blankets folding,
slippers swishing, a coffee pot bubbling.
"Kip, is that you?" Aunt Joan laughs.
He lunges for the lock.
"Open up," the full-bladder guests demand.
Frozen with Hannibal Lector terror,
Kip scans the bathroom for a secret tunnel
or a towel to tie a noose.
"Okay, bed check. We'll find out,"
screams the angry mob.
Shined with sweat, afraid to wipe,
Kip punches through a screen
and hurls his body through the open
window. Crashing to the moist dirt,

Kip hops up and begins to run
down the dewy road, pajamas
by his ankles, streams of white paper
flowing from his hand
like the surrendering French
Kip wonders what country
he's gonna live in next.

My Brother's Grateful Dead Records

I climb these attic stairs to listen
to my brother's Grateful Dead records.
I tip "Europe '72" and "Terrapin Station"
from their cases, then "American Beauty"
and "Go To Heaven." Then, I lower
the needle onto the scared grooves.

For a sound, the sound of a wooden bat
knocking balls into the crooked birch,
for fishing poles that scratch the shed
waiting for another day's perch.

For a voice, the voice of Mr. Douglass with his rake,
"I'm sure that's what those liberals want you to believe,"
he says from his sun-scorched face.
Jerry's guitar wails below our roof.

For a gasp, the gasp of a lucky hook shot
tossed from behind the fence. The sudden
scream of my best friend Steven
who slipped on the dock and broke his arm.
Mickey taps his hi-hats and strikes his toms.

For the cigarette tenors of liberal uncles
who railed against Nixon,
but loved Bernie Sanders.
Jerry goes off on an improv solo,
and in the attic I could see through time.

For the snickers of sneaky sisters
who hid dictionaries in their underwear,

and when discovered, they folded up their
Scrabble boards and slammed the screen door.

And Aunt Bee, at three o'clock,
already on her third Bloody Mary:
"Go ask your brother to fill a jam jar with crickets.
I want to hear them sing."

The Polar Bear Club

In thirty-three the price to join
The Chesterfield Golf Club
Was ten polar bear teeth.
Eight members teed off that year
And chased the scratch game.

The Mullins Society gathers in Des Moines.
Every March the lone survivors of lightning
Trade phone numbers, display
Scorched clothing and wonder
How a bald man grew hair
And a blind man gained vision.

Jesus syndrome runs rampant in Jerusalem.
Each year hundreds visit the desert city
Tour the stone churches, see the sun
Stuck in the sky like a blowfish,
When, suddenly, the Second Coming has arrived.

Clara's Grandmother collects light
Bulbs in their original boxes
On which she pencils in the date
The bulbs burned out.

When someone leaps off the escalator,
An x-ray pops out of the person beneath,
A probe is launched into unknown space,
Sisyphus steals a rest from his stone
And laughs as the moment becomes bronzed
In our collective mind.

It's reunion time in Rangeley.
Every ten years our class gathers
To share piss beer, feathered hair,
And life's largest blunders:

The time Kurt Quimby, high as a hippy,
Drove his pick-up through Eastlack's living room,
The Halloween students egged Chief Allen
And the dour drycleaner asked, "Do you want
Those pants dry cleaned or scrambled?"
Or the happy hour Mrs. Bysler opened
Doc's Tavern door, threw five suitcases inside
And screamed:"You want to be a free man!"

Each moment the suitcase flies,
Every time a tourist climbs on a soap box,
Or a golfer hands the cashier ten polar bear
Teeth: a flower blooms on a cactus
Somewhere, a lone beacon in a vast
Sahara of ice cream castle dust.

This grand opera of dunderheads and czars
Goes on. La Fayette still gallops through
Virginia, Marshall always runs the wrong
direction, My Brother's invention:
The suntan lotion shower booth lives,
And poor Icarus flaps his wings forever.

The whole horse is never lost,
When from Khorlo's tail
Stretches the violin's bow,
And life's sweet tune continues.

Evil Knieval

The sideburns like Elvis
Give it away: all daredevils
Are really cowards, but we
Love the statues they build:
The Parliament speeches
While the Luftwaffe drops bombs
On his head, the sixty home runs
After gallons of root beer, and
The broken bones at Caesar's Palace,
All life vests of a sort.
A communal transference takes place:
They whip our milksop nature
Till a scab forms our portrait,
Our shield, each lash
A brushstroke of self.
The flag leather suit
Over a Grand Canyon.
His custom Harley
Over a pool of sharks
Or the thirty Mack trucks
Back-to-back. In fifth
Grade I was astonished.
Fear grabbed a coward and made
A monument. I knowing very well,
Many tricksters triumphed
Where Evil failed,
But no one wants to talk
About them and their thin
Ephemeral scabs,
Just skin.

The Parent Season
For George E. Rowe Jr.

In morning's mirror I hear
my Dad's sermon: "Work hard.
Play hurt," he says behind a foam mask.
"The Dow is not as strong as Lehrer believes,
GM sales are off, unions might strike,
and that bastard Voelker may boost the prime."
And he did too, from key to key,
Christmas Eves and weekends.

From my brother's bed I hear
the door hinge's upward climb,
Dad's leather soles hurry down our walk
and his engine's slow fade.

Between the bathroom tiles
I see the razor's clean line
of shaved skin, splotched salmon,
puffed pressure of kids, bills,
and Seagram's. We never saw you still,
till now. Mom can retire the iron.
Key Bank can't recall another loan.
You will not peel another son
from a crumpled can
or charm another customer,
and we orphaned birds don boxing gloves
and jump from underneath your wings
to howling earth.

Through the Rosicrucian Halls of memory,
I recall the thud of shoulder pads,
the crack of helmets, and the lightning thighs

of Buckeye boys in Sunday's game.
On kitchen tables I see beehives of fruit
and pinwheels of meat. I hear soothing
voices of aunts and clinks of porcelain cups.
In our den I hear the strange voices of
unknown uncles, and the rare grimace
in a room of men.

On the cloth couch we hear the salesmen
trading stories, their suits shinier than
chrome fenders. On Sunday's sofa
we learned the gridiron plan, a bootleg turn,
a center sneak through the Wall Street Journal,
tracing the steps of Burnside's soldiers
marching to a distant Fredericksburg.

In your office, salesmen yield
like brides to your whip tongue.
Boys with chinstraps hope to be men.
Mud flies from cleats as you pet
strangers to sign contracts.
On your desk Vince Lombardi's locker room talk.
On your wall Ronald Reagan's portrait.

Now the quarterback has bruised ribs.
"Play hurt," you said. "Walk it off."
Too many rushing linemen
and foreign firms we could not see.
Uncle Jim consoles as you sign papers,
hand keys to a realtor,
and run to the sidelines.

The pigskin mythmakers remove
their helmets and limp to their lockers
like coyotes with chewed off paws,
their jerseys bathed in mud,

still minor league players,
seeking to stage struggle in a purer form.

And we tried, Dad. You running promotions,
Seeking to hire the best and brightest,
Expanding empires of finance, poaching
finance managers from rival dealers,
coaching boys on the dark art of sales,
and I, an eager son, who
looked for your white shoes
on the sidelines when I
caught a winning pass,
made the Dean's List,
helped Mom with a dish,
or shoveled the snow off our walk.
For one bathing suit summer we played
the King of Thebes. We stood
in Parliament's walnut chambers,
offered our blood, toil and tears
and discovered, after all,
we are all equal,
though we had Glastrons
and summer cabins.

The minister arrives in a rusted Tercel.
We close our mouths.
No need to talk. You can't hear.
For once, you could watch Sunday's game in silence.
We listen as the minister seeks
to straighten our bent faith.
But you never gave up, even when
GM pulled your number,
friend's sent their sons to others for advice,
Key Bank auctioned off our house.
We never learned the price.
But you dug deep an Argonne trench,

changed your tie, and sold another line:
custom vans, leather pelts, Electrolux.
Like Achilles dear friend Patrokolis,
You made another dash
through the gray suit jungle
before Zeus took your shield
and Hector smiled.

Every morning, Dad, your ghost
summons me as once a fallen
Dane to Elsinore's tower.
Behind a foam mask
I see the razor's clean line
and remember Hamlet's obligation:
to "work hard, play hurt"
and somehow return
all you gave away
for us.

And one parent season ends
and another begins
so many years later
in morning's mirror.

Today, the Dow shows signs of strength,
the parachutes can go back to the garage,
but still I'll drive to the office at 6 a.m.,
just in case. I heard that scoundrel Greenspan
is threatening to run off with Spring.

Aunt Grace

Part 1
Aunt Grace never ran from the minister,
weathered hailstorms of rice,
pinned tin can dragon tails to her Ford
or smudged five-story cake on her lover's mouth.

Instead, she waited for a Swedish prince
to burst joy like a ruby grape,
for voodoo champagne in Waterford glasses
on August evenings on a Beverly Farms porch,

clasping hands with King Gustav
who secretly loathed the throne
and loved the mojo berries in Aunty's garden.

Silver haired moon rocking in your Hitchcock
chair, hoarding those green creatures
of want, facing all the gasoline boys
and choosing to remain alone.

Part 2
Grace was frying eggs one cold November,
ironing dad's shirt at 5 a.m.
Mom was in McLean's again
with blue elephants swooping from the sky
like a Bf 109 Messerschmitt
diving down to grab Grandpa.

For years Aunt Grace captained seven sugar acid kids
for free. Little Vicky thought she was mom.
Mike and Paul streaked across the kitchen
while Grace peeled potatoes. She lowered her glasses,
not believing boys behaved that way.

Part 3

Grace shoveled the snow in the dark winter mornings,
defrosted her windshield, made the icy drive to our house
and glued back the shards of our eggshell home.
We gave her mixing bowls and blenders for Christmas.

The years passed, her glasses thick as coke bottles,
her face softer than the wind passing through
our curtains, Aunty only needed to smile and I realized
how precisely the world was built upon
the unacknowledged footsteps of strong women.

Part 4

Tonight, gazing at the Hancock Church steeple,
my fourth trip this week, unable to trade my dreams
of Princess Brigitte and her wik wik garden
for the ya ya girls at the Thirsty Scholar.

I wonder: Is that how Grace felt one cruel
November when Truman lived east of Missouri?
A young salesman on her porch with a diamond
held his breath, but she sent Grandma to the door.

How quietly he hid the gold ring
behind the socks in his top drawer,
like most of us, leaving our largest
disappointments unrecorded. Our chances,
so tenuous, they may have passed before birth.

Part 5

In ninth grade I learned so much when I saw Grace blush
at our door, where Mr. Krupp stood, fingers thick as sausages
from raising hothouse flowers. Like her powder blue dress,
I realized Grace was out of time, perfect for another century,
and our paths were set long before Dad met Mom
in saddle shoes with a junior high math book.

Part 6
Somewhere among the laundered stars I search
for Grace, still possibly watching, though no one
watched over you, alone, dying in a nursing home,
ankles swollen to grapefruits, metal walker by your bed.

How the world of bills and Monday morning sales
calls pulled us away, made us forget. Tonight I lean
against your headstone with my guitar, strumming
Don Mclean songs as a silver-haired moon
pokes its head through a velvet sky.

I could sing all night, rocking your headstone
back and forth, and you still wouldn't hear,
but somewhere amid the sawdust and blue quartz
of this jury-rigged universe, a particle might shift,
maybe just a quirk, back into alignment
and you might feel a little more loved.

Elvis Impersonators

I learned from my mother what
Elvis impersonators knew all along.
How, in the absence of diamonds, we
crave rhinestones, Las Vegas show tunes,
and fans like the nine planets circling the sun.
The practiced snarls, plastic surgery jaw,
and sideburns like boots, just a smorgasbord
of borrowed beams and alchemy—we mix
for gold, but all the audience ever hears
are the colors of our bruises. The human
mind nothing more than a dark closet
filled with a few fireflies: the way an uncle
argued for MacArthur, a big brother wrestled
down a ripped opponent, and the patent hip-shake.
The pretend Tupelo truck drivers sing,
but the gospel voice never comes. At every crossroad,
their shark-finned Cadillacs are parked
as they fumble with their maps: "What if
I switched to Vitalis, traded in my acoustic,
danced with Mandela, cockled with the roosters,
pilgrimed to Nepal?" they ask, sculpting
their hair in the mirror. The truth hits harder
than a drunk driver: we're all Elvis impersonators,
just less honest and haunted by a Memphis croon
that floats upwards and disappears in a tall bank
of cumulus, our infant hands still grasping
for the contours of his luminous voice.

Into The Untraveled

When I was four feet high
my dad drove a Lincoln large enough
for two parking spaces.
"You're rich," my friends said,
but I didn't know what that meant.
Then, Dad began coming home early
from work to watch Wall Street Week
and pour V.O. On the kitchen table,
bank notes and bills were piled
high as mom's fruit bowl.
"You should work," Dad said.
"A recession has begun." So, I wrapped
granddad's tie around my neck,
rode with him to work,
and performed surgery on
our balance sheet. Still the bill pile
overtook the fruit bowl.
"I don't know what to do?"
we confessed. The bank
auctioned off our house.
Chapter twelve ate our store.
"You keep to yourself, makes me feel alone,"
my wife said. "I'm sorry I don't know
what to do?" I said. She left
and took our kids and photo
albums. In the morning I shaved real
close till I bled. Then I slipped on
my best suit. "I've got a mailbox full too,"
my landlord said. So, I stuffed my trunk
with clothes, diplomas, and grandma's vase,
got in the car and drove.

Turning onto Route Four,
I released the gas and drifted
through the breakdown
lane. I didn't have a place to go.
There wasn't any business
and there wasn't any home.
"Just drive," I said and wiped
my face with granddad's tie.
"You are poor," a voice said
as the engine hummed.
"I know," I said, watching
the coffin-length yellow lines
bleeding into one long stripe
stretching down the highway
into the untraveled.

Ode To The Hanson Brothers From "Slapshot"

The duck-taped glasses are the clue:
how unfortunate to be born
beautiful. The fruitless years
with the face. Like a child's
trust-fund one cannot feel the gold
without blisters. But the Hanson Brothers
with their oily hair, camel-hump noses
and back-woods manners—all black
flags waving: "Onward!" Their hockey
sticks cracking opponent's helmets,
hooking skates, and the naughty cross
checks. In the theater we cheered
like Pompeii drunk at the Coliseum,
still caught in our Levi slumbers,
Dartmouth bumper stickers,
and Goldman Sachs bonuses,
still jousting with the peacocks
and all their blooming eyes
when all we really wanted
was to run
with the neighborhood dogs.

The Game Olin Timmins Missed the Open Goal

Only once did Olin's legs move
just the way his mind wanted.

Against Lisbon High at midfield,
Olin faked a striker left,

tapped the ball right,
and scampered down the sidelines

where a halfback slid,
but with his toe, Olin lifted the ball

and hurdled his flying spikes.
Dribbling towards the fullback,

Olin faked a pass and tapped the ball
through the fullback's legs

and circled around him. That's when
the goalie sprinted to the ball. Olin

did the same. Just before they collided,
Olin tapped the ball left,

sidestepped the charging goalie,
and gasped at the open goal.

But Olin took his eye off the ball,
saw glory early, swung his foot,
and the ball sailed past the open goal.

That night in the Hinman's boat house,
his teammates chugged a case of Heff talls.
Olin sat on the porch with Suzanne
as flames flickered on players' faces
and they coughed syrupy smoke.

"You dribbled past the whole
Team," Suzanne said as molten-colored
leaves slid down the tin roof.
"Yeah, a window opened,
but I couldn't crawl through."

At Stratton Lumber Olin sold
timber by the mile, pine boards
for lakeside homes. "Ninety-percent
of a sale is just showing up," his boss said.

Olin sold enough timber to reach Oregon
and back, sat in his own private office,
before sawmills from Quebec, logging
on Federal land, began dumping in the U.S.

At Doc Grant's, "Boom Boom" DeRaps
flung a beer in Olin's face. Olin's fist
struck his skull hard as an oak desk.
DeRaps's ring tore the flesh on Olin's cheek.
The juke box softened. Olin crumpled to the ground.

He woke as Coach Brewer and Chief Allen
escorted him into his house,
past Suzanne staring in her bath robe
and laid him on the couch.

That night, a blizzard from Quebec
dropped three feet of snow. Olin rose
at 4 a.m. filled his flask with warm milk,
and drove to the town garage.

In the parking lot at Rangeley High,
snow curled off his plow like ice cream scraped from a bowl.
Approaching a light pole, Olin faked left,
swerved right, and raced down the parking lot.

Approaching a snow bank, he tilted his plow
and pressed the gas and drove through the snow bank,
toppling a row of mailboxes. Swerving onto the road.
The snowplow zipped through the school gates

and sped up Dodge hill. With one eye on the road,
Olin veered North on Route 16.
Snowflakes thick as dimes
glowed in his headlights.

Shifting to fifth gear, the tires climbed onto
the snow's surface. Olin raised the plow
and the truck lifted above the virgin snow.

Floating over the tops of spruce,
the truck plowed through a cloud bank
and emerged to an ink blue sky,
the truck's silhouette framed in the Vaseline moon.

In panic, Olin buckled his seat belt.
Why was his Dad up here in his tan coat smiling?
Why was his brother's crumpled Corvette
and his high school soccer ball up here?

In his rear view mirror he took in the earth.
"Harmless, really. Just a cobalt marble
in a child's pocket." Olin opened the cab door,
swung his leg faster than an axe
and gave the ball a mighty kick.

What would Coach Brewer think in the morning,
pulling into Rangeley High, a steaming mug

in his hand, a peek hole scraped through the ice
on his windshield, and a parking lot full of snow?

In June a surveyor found the plow truck
in the woods near Kennebago,
oddly, twenty miles from the nearest road.
The front end punched in like a paper bag,
blood and hair on the windshield,
Olin's half-full thermos, but no clothes,
no bones that wolves might have chewed.

That summer in a marsh three miles away.
A canoe passed over the remains of a man,
six-foot-two, mid-thirties, but no teeth to I.D.,
flesh flaking off his body like the Dead Sea scrolls.

Meanwhile, Suzanne answered phones
for Morton Lumber. Canadian Geese
flew down from Lac Megantic same as
they always did, and in Chief Allen's pocket
a citation for a stolen truck rested.

From her porch, Jan Eustis, beer-blind
From a twelve-pack, chanced to look
up in the sky as a meteor arced across
the Rangeley night, passed through a cloud,
and slammed into the soccer field.
"The sky rained headlights," she claimed.

No one listened, but that August
Coach Brewer, laying chalk
for the autumn season, wondered
why a six foot hole was dug
in the back of the visiting team's goal.

The Pretend Man

Hey, Dad, do you remember me?
I'm the kid who broke his arm
when I fell from a tree,
threw a football though your skylight
and blamed it on John.

Hey, Dad, did you ever know?
I read Charlotte's Web ten times.
When I scored a winning goal,
I felt so high when I
saw you crack a smile.

Now I'm lying on my bed,
staring at the ceiling,
hoping that some meaning will
emerge from all these feelings.

I ate four packs of cough drops,
missed the sink when I got sick.
Your truck rolled in Granny Pond
when I forgot to pull the break.
My first job out of college lasted three days.

Now I drive a plow for the town
and I have failed much worse than you,
I think your habit's okay,
though nothing can bring back Mom
or her dream-filled wedding day.

Would I do the same if I could find a wife?
Say, Dad, how did you get Mom to fall in love?

Now I'm lying on my bed,
staring at the ceiling,
hoping that some meaning will
emerge from all these feelings.

How did you get people to love you
so much, and why didn't you like me?
I never spoke unless spoken to,
your golden rule, and now mine too.

Hey, Dad, do you know who I am?
A pajama-clad kid inside a pretend man
just like you. Why do you stare
in the mirror with such hate?
Did Grandpa say you're no good?
I think you're great.

Eric Russo the "Italian Tank" From Burlington

At my sister's graduation party I told my big brother, two guys threw beer on us by the train tracks—bottles too. "Let's check it out," Donk said to Russo, my cousin's boyfriend from Burlington. Russo was a house and wore a handlebar moustache. We hopped in Donk's Nova and drove to the train tracks.

In the dark, two guys sat on a log, drinking soldiers. Donk asked, "What's going on?" and kicked the big fella in his face. The guy barely flinched and came at Donk with a bottle. Donk lifted him off his feet.

The two fell onto the tar and rolled around. Donk grabbed the guy's hair and slammed his head against the tar till he let the bottle go. Donk's knee flew into his crotch. Yet, the guy managed to roll Donk off and get on his feet.

We got a good look at who he was. Jeff Tossy, just paroled from Walpole for pummeling a kid in his own kitchen. Donk hesitated, but Russo stared. "What the hell you looking at?" the guy said.

Russo kicked off his clogs and they went at it. I'd never seen a man throw jabs so fast, and there was blood all over the guy's face, but the sick unit kicked Russo in the nuts. Russo bent over, wondering if he was ever gonna have kids. "Give up?" the guy called.

"You're not going anywhere," Russo warned. The two circled each other. I heard the crack of Russo's ring against the guy's skull. (I was twelve and didn't want anyone to get hurt, but there's no messing with the way humans think.) A little more dancing. Then, the guy said, "I've had enough." So, we piled into Donk's Nova and drove back to the graduation party.

A few years after Donk's car wreck, Paul and I saw the guy playing football on the Green. He noticed us and walked over, his arms bigger than Lyle Alzado's. I thought he would go back to Walpole and us to the Mass General. But honoring our youth, the guy only looked at us and smiled. "Sometimes you bite the bear, sometimes the bear bites you," he said and threw the football to his friend.

    Twenty years later, I bumped into Russo at my cousin's. He wore the same handlebar moustache, was slightly bald, but built like an Italian tank. Said he missed my brother, that he was a lawyer, and lived in California. I don't remember what else we said, but the puzzled look he gave me when I hugged the big bastard just for still being there, and he must have thought I'd lost my marbles.

Handing Out Apples on Halloween Night in Merriam Hill, Massachusetts

My wife's at the door with a bushel of apples.
"Those poor toothless adults," she says.

I drop popcorn balls into pillow cases
of bumble bees with panty-hose wings

and cherub pumpkins with legs pulling their parents.
Up our walk comes a grizzly bear with fake fur

and a lion with a goldenrod tail made from a hanger,
unlike adults trapped in our bodies, clawing our organs

with ulcers, cancer, and coronaries. Oh, I hate Halloween.
I could never figure out who I wanted to be

and Abe Lincoln's hat keeps falling off my head.
My dog once swallowed a bee, shook wildly,

then spit it out. But in my pajamas, fur-lined slippers,
and a tray of sweets, I can't find my own costume.

I could buy my kids all the chocolate they want
but something deeper propels them. I will order

them to pour their candy on the bed to check for
hidden pills and razor blades. I won't mention

the false promise: one second on the lips and no afterlife.
In ninth grade, my buddies and I fired bottle rockets

at John Parker's statue. We couldn't figure out
what else to do. In our yard, a sugar maple gasps

in bright salmon. My wife and I stand under an archway,
serving apples, throwing shadows twice our height.

A president, a thief, a frog, and a ghost, their parents in tow,
parade across our grass. I see the sureness of each foot

moving through the air, firm and resolute, and there I am,
standing in my own doorway, waiting to exist.

Subconscious Thoughts of a Celtics' Fan

High in the radio rafters in Boston Garden,
Johnny Most swills a cola and presses his lips
to the moist microphone...

Sunken on a couch in Merriam Hill,
Robby Rowe sets down his Heff tall
and leans towards the radio.

"...Greer looks to make an inbound pass.
He looks to Chamberlain who's covered
by Russell. Twelve seconds left. Celtics
up by one. Sixers with a chance to take home
the gold ball. Greer shifts left. He looks to
Walker. Havilcek playing a bit off. Greer
flings the ball out deep. Havilcek charges
towards Greer. He steps in front. He steals it!
Havilcek stole the ball! He passes it off to Jones.
It's all over! It's all over! Jones gives it back.
John Havilcek has just stolen the ball and led
the Boston Celtics to a world–Rowe steals it!
Rowe stole the ball! Robby Rowe has just stolen
the ball! He dribbles down court, fakes out
Chamberlain, and lays it up smooth as butter.
Celtics win the world championship! Rowe
is being mobbed by fans! Celtics win!
Rowe wins! It's a bee hive at the Garden, folks.
The house that Rowe built. It's all over! It's all over!"

Christmas Caroling on Oars Island

    My father, two-hundred-and-fifty pound car dealer,
who fed eight kids and two hounds with the phrase,
"I know what you sold last month,
how many tires can you roll this month?"
twists a tray of ice.

    My sister, part-time minister, heavyweight Jesus
champion, slides the turkey into the oven
and mentions: "Last night Scott's ghost hovered
above my bed in circles of angelic light."

    My cousin, Amway dealer, landscaper to Marblehead's
elite, who begins each sentence with, "I hear what
you're saying but-", slices pumpkin bread.

    And my mother, beehive-haired, ex-Miss
New Hampshire, who tried to modify our behavior with,
"What would the neighbors think?"
purees a batch of poppy seed dressing.

    At the dinner table the same routine: we stare
in a circle of moon plates, cornbread stuffing,
three-bean salad, and acorn squash. There are words
we want to say, but sounds slip from our tongues
and diffuse into silence.

    The milk stout is sweet, but cannot charm
the notes from my belly. Instead, my eyes skip from dad's
hands to my uncle's beard and grandma's mad hair.
I cannot look into my sister's eyes—she knows.
To connect would mean to acknowledge.

Dad slides a knife across the turkey's back.
Mom scoops cranberry sauce and clove poached pears
onto our plates. Something hangs above our chandelier
like frozen apples on December trees unable to fall.
The deer starving in winter cannot reach them.

　　　After dinner Mom enters with a stack of music books.
We pull on our coats and step into the night. Waves of
snow roll off the sea. My sister points to the Heisey's house,
but their windows are dark as a closed mill. We walk to
the Borgman's where a bulb glows in the yard.

　　　On their steps we part our hymns and strain
to keep pitch with Mom, who sings in the church choir.
"Angels we have heard on high…" The knob doesn't budge.
"Let's go home," my brother says.
"Shush!" Mom herds us to the next house.

　　　In the Blackmer's driveway, Mom hums a C.
We begin to sing, but a wave of snow drowns our song.
"Deck the halls with boughs of holly, fa la la la la…"
My tone is flat and I can't find the pitch.
"This isn't fun," I say.
"It will be in memory," my uncle replies,
snow collecting in his beard.
"Wait until they ask us for egg nog."

　　　The next four homes are licorice dark.
We hurry to the Van Dyne's where seven cars
fill the drive. Mom hums an E.
"O come, O come, Emmanuel, and ransom captive Israel…"
Caught between two alto's, my larynx cracks.
"Rejoice, rejoice, Emmanuel." Consonants drop
from our frozen tongues and vanish in the snow.
No one presses their face to the glass.

We traipse towards home, our faces pale ponds of ice.
On the Scribner's lawn, we gather by a pine tree
strung with lights. "Everyone knows this song," says Mom.
We close our hymns. My sister hums a G.

"Silent night, holy night. All is calm, all is bright..."
The monotone is easy. I clasp my sister's hand.
My legs are frozen logs. "...round yon virgin
mother and child..." Our voices blend together
as we wait for a porch light and trays of hot chocolate.

Snow thick as dimes begins to fall.
We huddle close. "Holy infant so tender and mild."
Dad drapes his long scarf around our necks
as our voices drift off in the speckled night
to a metronome of black waves lapping the shore
as the last bit of blood drains from our cheeks.

The Night Liam McGarvey Egged Lexington

Folks still argue the reasons why.
Whether a few synapse misfired
in Liam's brain or a girl Fed Ex'd
back a ring. What we know,
at three a.m. Liam McGarvey
kicked off his sheets, snuck down
the stairs, and grabbed a box of
grade-A bullets. As his mom snoozed
on the couch, Liam slipped through
the screen door and raced down Elm
Street in striped pajamas and slippers,
painting the town eggshell white.
Selectman Barnes heard a string of
thuds just after Leno. Mrs. Crothers
swears she saw a dress. Either way,
when Lexington woke, crushed shells
and yolk dripped down their wood
shingles. While the sandman performed
his magic, Liam was lobbing eggs
over the elms to the Barton's, a house
he once threw news. Already two homes
away when he heard the triple splat.
Swimming through the velvet night
past the Scruton's lawn, hurling Nolan
Ryan fast balls, seeing the lights flash on
and confused faces pressed against the
glass. Soaring past the lilac houses,
hopping across the roofs of Mercedes,
if only he were running track, at this
moment, the fastest in the state.
On Merriam Hill, a neighbor found a

sneaker. "What kind of man derives
strength from this?" Turning onto
Main Street, whooping like a college
football drunk, Liam sprinted to Key Bank
and launched eggs behind a birch.
Running down the street, while a Vaseline
moon hung in a gin sky, Liam lobbed a
half-dozen at the mayor's house.
Then, kicking his legs through a field,
leaping over a hedge, scaling a chain link
fence, feeling warm his blood mix with
cool air, Liam ran to I-95, waved his thumb
down the mica chip highway, and was gone,
probably picked up by an eighteen wheeler
and raced though the Midwest
on his way to Tibet.

The tongues at Fitzy's Donuts click,
professors write their books, neighbors
scrub their shingles and wonder:
Was it the bank that took his parent's house?
The game he missed the winning shot?
The protein strands in his double-helix?
"Maybe Liam needed a myth,"
Mrs. Crothers guessed, "to give
freedom a form." Seeing how the
world hinges on things small as a
five o'clock shadow, an Austrian's
rejection from art school, the current
steering Moses' basket, and the fleas
on the back of a rat, one must ask:
Why did Liam McGarvey egg Lexington?

The dumpsters continue to fill with yesterday's
newspapers, the topics at Fitzy's live a few hours,
but there Liam goes sprinting down Main Street,
painting the town egg shell white.

In Praise of Cheap Shots

      I love the two players reaching
for the same ball and an elbow biffs
the ribs, helmet to helmet in the mud
with a lineman's spit swinging from his mask,
the rugby field when a hooker mutters,
"flounder breath." To win is not enough.
Take The ten thousand meters when
a champion is passed, a yawn expands
the drama and a worthy opponent always
runs faster. I'm talking about the pale orb
at the cell's center, the one that cries out:
"an éclair for a spine won't do."
"New York," I once heard a gentleman say,
"ten million people rude as hell in one place—
I love New York." And if you're trading
stocks, please, some inside information
for my personal freedom. In each foul lies
this kernel: they're cross-checking to
vault themselves to Avalon. So more
mud, not just the garlands that make
our heads swell, 'cause through
the mud rise sunflowers that bloom
into gold medals. Besides, the refs
are never around.

The Wrong Guy

In Rusty's Convenience Store some guy bumped into
my soda and had the sack to say, "Watch it, pal."
I was with Kendra, so I arc'd a loogy over the
lobster tank, above their clicking claws gauging
the green shells of their friends. The loogy
landed on his cheek. He didn't like that.
"Let's take it outside." He put down a six-pack.
"I'll rip your head off and stuff it down your neck,"
I said. (But I was kind of nervous. He was jacked.)
"Oh you're a big man, I'd like to see your tax returns."
Next thing I know we're dancing on the mica chipped
highway, junior pavement ballet stars, but I was
losing patches of skin on the tar the size of Texas.
I know I shouldn't have run my mouth, but I can steal
more street signs than any senior at Merriam High.
The guy bullrushed me. My knee flew up in his face.
For some reason, I started thinking about my brother.
Donk could stick to you like glue, and if he thought
someone was a snob, he'd bullrush them and smoosh
his face in the grass. Now we're up on our feet. The guy's
throwing haymakers. I'm weaving and bobbing. Suddenly,
the guy transforms into my boss, then my eighth grade
nemeses—Stan Kluko—and then my dad. I'm still
looking for my first hug. Then, Grandpa. Pretty soon,
I didn't know who the heck I was fighting. So, I'm said
I'm sorry and walked away. Life's like that—we're always
Fighting the wrong guys and there's plenty of us and there's
Plenty of them, and there's still more jackholes than toilets.

Strip Poker with the Carson Sisters

Mr. Graham's at the auction buying cars.
Mrs. Graham's on the porch hanging clothes.
I'm on the third floor with Len, Myles,
Kara, plus the Carson sisters
in three sweaters, nine socks, and five belts,
with a pack of airline cards.
Len deals face up. Lara escapes with Jack,
but the losing hands come.
"It's just skin," Myles reasons.
Divine peach velvet vellum.
"Show it to me! Show it to me!"
the Carson sisters demand.
A bluebell unfurls in the garden.
I remove my boxers and look down.
Is it nakedness or my nakedness alone?
Lara, down to her bra, draws a three.
The air is sweet with elm leaves.
She sprints from the room.
"Cheater," we call, but cannot pursue.
The June sun warps the air to clear ribbons.
Ginny's underwear drops down to the braided rug.
The pine boards between us began to stretch.
My distant feet and this weird world.
My boyhood bliss gone. This treasonous body
now dependent upon others.
 "What in Christ's name are you two doing?"
Mrs. Graham stands in the doorway.
I reach for a blanket. Ginny runs behind a chair.
The Carson sisters giggle.
Next morning I woke in my bed,
my cleats were on, Dad was old,
and some curious race had begun.

Scenes From The Dentist Chair

What do you think, Trina?
Monday in the dentist's chair,
Novocain in your cheek like ginger ale,
Dr. Harrington in a surgeon's uniform
Grinding a tooth the color of old news?

Trina, with your mouth crow-barred open,
Your hands squeezing the vinyl cushion,
Your jogging shoes wiggling,
How do your notions change?
When the drill find a nerve,
Only time can deliver us.

Do you picture a Civil War infirm
Where a stick in the mouth sufficed?
When a bayonet slice was enough reason
For the saw's slow cough
Through bones the color of Easter.
The gauze soldiers cry from their stumps,
"How small your tooth is!"
"Go ahead," you tell him,
"Yank the damn thing out!"
But Harrington only grins.
"Sooner than later, you'll need to chew."

Trina, when you sleep in a hospice,
Read poems to the bald children,
Tell them why they shouldn't be afraid,
When you fly to Bergen-Belsen,
Stand in concrete showers
Or sift through boxes of gold teeth

Still chattering, but no longer with bodies
To give them use, does our naked
Wedding ring finger still matter?

I suppose the corn field's green flowering tongues
Will continue their photo magic,
And the ivory-winged wood bills
Will still beat their wings south,
But the carbon shadow on the x-ray
Of our failed love clings. So, snap
Me a twig, and press my teeth down.

And the dentist returns his bits to their shelf.
Your tooth filled with a new composite
He assures is better. "Have a spool of floss."
Harrington bows, then vanishes. And I'm back
In the busy sunlight, the traffic's larceny
Of horns and tires.

What do you think, Trina?
"Speak! You never speak."
"I don't know," she says,
"Besides you're too busy talking,
Always drilling your own cavities."
For one insufficient moment we paused.
Isn't that the way love always is.
All we can do, is put on our germ proof masks
and see another patient.

Traveling to Darian's

Pedaling my bicycle at dusk
through Portland's warehouse
district, bumping over cobblestones,
traveling to Darian's past shoe mills
abandoned, floating in the dark,
crunching sand past loading docks
like surprised mouths and vacant
car lots where a few green blades
squeeze through the tar.
"This is you," a voice whispered.
I shook my head. "But Darian,
my friends." I pedaled past a
collapsed roof. "This is you,"
a voice followed. "But my sales
team reached our target. I raced
down the hill. "You." The voice
caught up. Suddenly nauseous,
I peddled to a dock, sat on the
rubber ledge, and watched
the remnants of day dissolve
in a blue blanket. She was right.
I was traveling to Darian's
faithless we could solve
the riddle of our separateness.
All these years while life's clothing
faded, we clung to the world
we knew, peddled faster
for promotions, respect from peers,
acting refined for strangers,
hoping to attract someone who
waltzed finer than Astaire, swam
faster than Spitz. Now, before
silhouettes of shoe mills,

for some strange reason I think
of you little Mikey. How you
followed me home from school.
How, with my friends, I threw
snowballs, drove you away.
How quizzically you looked back,
not yet weak enough to know why
the world was such a mean place.
But still you snuck in my room.
Each night under blankets we watched
Gilligan play the fool, the Bionic Man
outrun a car. Years later, we understood
why. And still I threw my stick under
your skate when you stole the puck
and you cried home to Mom
with a bloody chin, and I hated my
self twice. Now, I drive two hours
to visit. We stand on your porch
and talk about Montana. You already
on your seventh beer and one late
mortgage face me with that same
blank stare I saw so many years
earlier and I wonder: if only I could have
been a little bit bigger of a brother
maybe you could have caught
that bionic man. Tonight, pedaling
my bike past blocks and blocks of
abandoned mills and brick warehouses
filled with Lord knows what, traveling
to Darian's not believing in anything,
I come to you, little Mikey, following
me home, wanting then what I seek now
and I realize I am Gilligan the fool,
and we are windowless shoe mills,
abandoned and shells of what
we once were.

Brett Douglass Swims The English Channel

It's okay if you try in the day,
Swim with an escort vessel,
Apply Vaseline thick as toothpaste
All over your body, but that's not
the way Brett Douglass tried.

We were on a rugby field in Cornwall
When Dewey realized his most radiant move;
Five forwards were left on the grass
And Dewey untouched in the try-zone
Trying to bronze the moment.

We went back in our formation.
It was men's league after all.
I told Douglass: "Get in line."
"And do what?" He peeled his jersey off,
Ran towards the shore, stepped down
A few dozen stairs and entered the gray waves.

This kind of swimming is an art:
To move through water with least resistance,
To shave your eyebrows and hot wax your skin.
His buddy sped to town and borrowed a rowboat.
Jill wired a ferry. I dropped the ball,

Almost fell down the stairs, and joined Brett
In the Channel. His long back surging forward.
His full-kick breaking the surface
As dusk dropped a cobalt blanket.

After what seemed a lifetime and
barely a glimpse of land, I circled back.
My last vision of Brett, or was it lost otter
poking through the water, was a human head
surging through the endless gray waves.

The truth is I never saw Brett's move.
Whether he head-faked the whole team,
or he burst through a hole in a crowd of
players or three defenders slipped—I don't know,
but in my gut, Brett popped from his body
to pilot the air with the ease of water.

The Blue Sling

At 2 a.m., when Congress adjourned,
Senator Lane amended a bill;
"All persons shall tie their left arms
Behind their backs." Federal tailors
Crafted a blue sling. At first simple tasks:
To pack a suitcase or shovel winter snow
Took twice the time and new routines
Developed: Vendors gave out hot-dogs
Then took bills; Parents hoisted Easter
Hams together, used quinders to scoop snow.
Decades passed, arms bound themselves.
Left-handed baseball gloves vanished.
Guitars were sent to museums. Softball
Fields were halved. On occasion, photos
Of Rogers and Astaire dancing, and Ted
Williams' barber pole swing surfaced.
"What an ugly appendage," the crowds
Yelled. At theaters, "The Man with Two Arms"
Frightened moviegoers. Still, in unguarded
Moments, when lifting a laundry bin or
Pushing out a snowbound car, a current
Passed through the dry riverbeds of their
Memories, a whirligig swirled around
Their mind's periphery. Somewhere there
Was a method of less resistance, a way to
Build all the glass palaces unbuilt, and to
Un-burn the Library of Alexandria. So, a sculptor
Eyes a slab of marble and asks, "What is two-
Handed possibility or blue slinglessness? What
Parts of human beings were roped-off
And why? Forgive these glass eyes, they
Cannot tell a kerosene lamp from the sun.

Conversations From a Barber's Chair

Morley, how quickly it grows!
Just last month I warmed the red cushion.
You snipped my Faucet curls
and saved a lock for Mom's jewelry box,
but here we are again.

"Whose head this time?" the barber asks.
DeGaulle's? Saint John's? What traits
do you want? Can't do much with the face."
But all this work diffused in a gust of wind.
How would Elvis look in Hoover's part?

Morley, I hear when a man dies
his hair still grows. Just think
acres and acres of uncut hairdos.
"Where shall we begin?" he asks.
"I'm not sure. I can't hear
what the dead are saying."
"You must have clues?"
"My mind is blank for a gel
and wave that mirrors my soul."

The natives are fleeing our cameras,
Morley, chanting heathen Rosaries,
shielding their eyes, reaching for
their spears. When a river divides
the water dawdles in small streams.

"Give me a moon Jell-O. Make me feel
like a hummingbird," I ask.
"You're freaking me out," he says.

"Morley, stop telling me there's something
wrong with Congress. There's
something wrong with me. I can't pass
a mirror without pausing. Every time
I look a Cardinal flies from my hair."

"But what if boogers collect or your tie's
crooked? Plus, there's so little to go on
when each laugh contains ten voices,
and every hand shake a different desire."

All these herkimer diamonds, chocolate tombstones,
protein monuments. What was Sampson's problem?
What's the Dali Lama trying to do?
Pluck out my eyes, Morley.
I can't tell fool's gold from the sun.

"Cut my hair so short that I won't return.
"But what will you do with all the free time?"
"I want to make sure I look good in my casket."

Morley, the scissors are snipping.
Gray curls are dropping like oak leaves.
Younger customers are waiting.
"Your Grandma's in line."
"But she won't remarry."
"Your Brother's here with newborn photos. You're single."
"Cut me like him, I guess."

Barber poles are spinning
in every town. "Sometimes, Morley,
I wish your scissors would just… "

Freedom on The Fringes For Francis Layne
(Le Poème Morte)

Poised and comfortable on a couch
in the Parker House lobby,
a python of smoke rising
from my Marley cigar,
I cross my legs smugly,
assured of my man
enough to payroll a closet queen
to alien free worlds
in petite gestures:
petting the velvet couch,
undressing guests with my eyes
peering down the blood-red
carpets for my prey.
I smirk at the contradiction:
to them I am a harmless femme.
A suited man swaggers across my eyes.
Fugamo shoes and a Hilltop suit!
He feigns not to notice.
(I sense he sincerely doesn't.)
From my cushion, I rise
and hurry down the hall
like Bella Lugosi with diarrhea.
He turns.
I turn.
He opens a door.
I do the same.
He sees my spy-like austerity.
Now, he cares. It is too late
Rome will be sacked by Goths,
the Library of Alexandria burned to ash.

In the bathroom we are alone.
He breaths like a train.
"All those weekends on Nantucket
and twelve-point cotton shirts
still led you to me," I say,
laughter oozing like lava
from my chest. I clasp
his sweaty face with my palm
and drag him into a stall.
I throw his head against the tiles
and kick his spongy ribs
with my pointy shoes,
one extra time for Enron.
Shrieks fill the bathroom
with songs of a dying cat.
I Seize his wallet
and shred the filth
on his pink patrician bum.
I flush his Mastercards
down the toilet.
"I exist," I shout as I exit.
Strolling down the hall,
I comb my hair with my fingers
and whistle with old boy ease.
Back on the couch, I blow
smoke rings at patrons,
comforted with the thought
that they might be next.

Biography

Robert Rowe grew up with seven brothers and sisters in Lexington, Massachusetts, where his Dad ran a Chevy dealership. Rowe attended high school in Rangeley, Maine, spending his free time playing guitar, hiking, reading, and ski racing. During his senior year, his high school ski team won the state championship. Rowe studied writing at the University of Maine, Farmington with Kenneth Rosen, Wesley McNair, and Bill Roorbach. Later, Rowe studied songwriting and drama at UCLA. He received an M.F.A. in Creative Writing from the University of Massachusetts, Amherst, studying with John Edgar Wideman, Noy Holland, James Tate, Mary Reufle, and Dara Wier. After college, he worked as an English teacher, car salesman, musician, and dressman. In 1995 Rowe founded the New England Journal of Poetry and Fiction. In 2017 he co-founded the Rowe School of Writing. His short story "The Violin Player" appeared in the *Sandy River Review*. In 2108 his novel GARAGE SONGS was a #1 Best Selling New Release on Amazon. Rowe lives in Natick, Massachusetts with his wife Marisa and three sons.

Photo by Holly Hinman

Acknowledgements

My name is listed on the cover, but this novel has hundreds of poets, authors, and lyricists. Any utterance, quip, sales pitch, lyric, poem, late-night philosophical rant, riff, sing-songy phrase, putdown, novel, sermon, biography, song, magazine newspaper or website article, coach's game day urgings, movie scene, sports commenter's phrase, bedside epiphany, business journal, and high school game of one-upmanship that I've ever read or heard influenced me as I wrote this collection of poems. Foremost, thanks to Michael Jones at Bellhorn Press. Thanks to my peers at the University of Massachusetts Amherst MFA Program: Noah Blaustein, Tom Kealey, Carry Comer, Kendra Borgmann, Ben Alsup, David Roderick, Mathew Kashorik, Robyn Heisey, Jon Haner, Nick Montramanaro, and Mathew Zapruder. Thanks to my poetry and fiction professors and mentors: Kenneth Rosen, John Edgar Wideman, Noy Holland, James Tate, James Haug, Wesley McNair, Shahid Aga Ali, Dara Wier, Mary Ruefle, and Bill Roarbach. Thanks to the poets: James Wright, Gerard Manley Hopkins, Elizabeth Bishop, Philip Levine, Walt Whitman, A. L. Tennyson, Edna St. Vincent Millay, Langston Hughes, Robert Frost, Gregory Corso, Russ Sargent, A.E. Robinson, Joan Crothers, Andrew Marvell, Jay Davis, Theodore Roethke, and to playwrights Eugene O'Neil and Arthur Miller. Thanks to comedians Billy Wilder, Bob Marley, Dan Aykroyd, Douglass Kenney, Chris Miller, and John Belushi.

New Voices in Fiction Series

Bellhorn Press is accepting submissions of unpublished novels, plays, and screenplays for our New Voices in Fiction Series. Submissions should contain strong elements of comedy, but may also be dramas with comedic situations, coming-of-age stories, tragicomedies, philosophical comedies, or stories with elements of irony, youthful indiscretions, pretensions unmasked, and more. Screenplays should be movie-length or three episodes of a television series. We are looking for well-written and well-crafted manuscripts that have the potential to appeal to a broad audience of readers, viewers, and producers. For more information contact:

Bellhorn Press
P.O. Box 812142
Wellesley, MA 02482
Website: bellhornpress.com
Phone: 781-214-0425
Email: info@bellhornpress.com

www.ingramcontent.com/pod-product-compliance
Lightning Source LLC
Chambersburg PA
CBHW081347040426
42450CB00015B/3341